I0823239

Nature's Rivals

Honeybees vs. Hornets

JOANNE MATTERN

Mitchell Lane
PUBLISHERS

Parent and Caregiver Tips for Creating Nonfiction Readers

The high-interest topics in the *Nature's Rivals* series are sure to get your young reader excited about reading nonfiction. While exploring a fascinating subject, your reader will be introduced to new concepts, facts, ideas, and vocabulary.

Tips for Reading Nonfiction

Talk about Nonfiction

Explain that nonfiction books provide facts about real-world topics. When readers read nonfiction, they gain a rich understanding of the world. They build background knowledge that provides a foundation for learning and academic success.

Look at the Parts

This book contains the following helpful features. Share the purpose of each feature with your reader.

Photos, Captions, and Graphic Aids

The photos, captions, charts, maps, and other graphic aids in nonfiction texts contain a wealth of information. Help your reader identify different ways information can be displayed.

Sidebars

These extra tidbits of information help satisfy readers' curiosity and expand their knowledge.

Table of Contents

Located at the front of the book, this list shows the big ideas within the text and the page numbers where they can be found.

Glossary

Located at the back of the book, the glossary defines key words and phrases that are related to the topic. These words and phrases can be found in the text in **bold** type.

Comprehension Questions (Fact Check)

Multiple-choice questions help readers self-check to make sure they understand what they read.

Index

Located at the back of the book, the index is an alphabetical list of topics and the page numbers where they can be found.

With a little help and guidance, your reader will be on their way to enjoying and learning from nonfiction books.

Mitchell Lane
PUBLISHERS
mitchelllanepub.com

2001 SW 31st Avenue
Hallandale, FL 33009

First Edition, 2026.
Author: Joanne Mattern
Designer: Jen Bowers
Editor: Tricia Hoffman

Series: Nature's Rivals
Title: Honeybees vs. Hornets / by Joanne Mattern

Hallandale, FL : Mitchell Lane Publishers, [2026]

Library bound ISBN: 979-8-89260-601-1
Paperback ISBN: 979-8-89260-613-4
eBook ISBN: 979-8-89260-608-0

PHOTO CREDITS
Shutterstock: Steidi, cover and 1, MOH NOR ROMADHON, cover and 1; Roman Marusew, 3; Daniell Avraum, 4, Riccardo Zamboni, 4; Mehes Daniel, 5; Fiona M. Donnelly, 6; Poring, 7, Que Sera Sera, 7; TravelPhotoSpirit, 8; Ikonoklast Fotografie, 9; Anthony King Nature, 10, Smeerjewegproducties, 10; Valeriy Karpeev, 11, 28; Ruth Swan, 12; Prontasov AN, 13, Perutskyi Petro, 13; ThomasLENNE, 14; Vasyichenko, 15; Michele.Ursi, 16, 28; Maksim Safaniuk, 17; saiglobalnt, 18; Ashan Turan Menekay, 19; Animaflora PicsStock, 20; Maksim Safaniuk, 21; Que Sera Sera 22; s.tokarev, 23, Chris Moody, 23; nonupperuct, 24; Lipatova Maryna, 25, 26; Anthony King Nature, 27; Peter Hermes Furian, 28

Contents

On the Hunt

The honeybee flies from flower to flower. She is gathering **nectar** and **pollen** to bring back to the hive. It is an ordinary day for the bee and her companions. But they don't know they are in terrible danger.

A hornet has been following the honeybees. As they fly back to the hive, the hornet follows them. She watches the bees go inside their home. Then, the **scout** secretly marks the hive with a special smell. The bees don't know that their home has become a target for a deadly enemy.

Other hornets smell the mark that the scout has left outside the honeybee hive. A group of them fly toward the beehive. They plan to enter the hive, kill the bees, and steal their honey.

But the bees have noticed the hornet's marker. It's time for them to get ready for battle. The honeybees gather in a big ball inside the hive. They **vibrate** their wings. The vibrations create a lot of heat. When the hornets fly inside, they are in terrible danger. What will happen next?

Life as a Honeybee

Honeybees and hornets are both insects. They live all over the world.

Honeybees live in big groups called colonies. Each colony has three kinds of bees. These are workers, drones, and a queen.

Each hive has just one queen. Her only job is to lay eggs. A queen bee can lay up to 2,000 eggs a day! A drone's only job is to mate with the queen so she can lay eggs.

Crowded House

There can be more than 20,000 worker bees in a hive. There are several hundred drones.

Like their name says, workers bees work! They take care of the eggs and **larvae**. They clean the hive. They fly out to bring back pollen and nectar for the other bees to eat. They use the nectar to make sweet honey. One beehive can produce up to two pounds (0.9 kg) of honey per day.

Keep It Simple

All worker bees are female. All drones are male.

Birds and other animals like to eat honeybees. But the bee has a good defense. Each worker bee has a sharp **stinger** in its **abdomen**. The stinger is attached to a **venom sac**. A honeybee's sting is very painful. The sting swells up. It itches a lot. If an animal is stung many times, it could even die.

One and Done

A worker honeybee can only sting once. The stinger pulls out some of the bee's **organs**, so it dies.

Deadly Hornets

Most honeybees are peaceful creatures. Hornets ... not so much! A hornet is a kind of wasp. Wasps are longer and thinner than bees. But a hornet is a super-sized wasp. These creatures can be up to two inches (5 cm) long. That's about as long as a large paper clip. A honeybee is less than half that size.

Like bees, each hive, or colony, has three kinds of hornets. These are workers, drones, and a queen. But there are only a few hundred hornets in a colony.

Hornets eat fruit and tree sap. But they also eat other insects. A hornet can be a fierce **predator**. And one of their favorite foods is honeybees.

Hornets also like sweets. They often attack beehives to get the tasty honey inside.

Hornets have stingers, just like bees do. But a hornet's stinger is longer and sharper. Its venom is more powerful than a bee's. And hornets don't die when they sting. A hornet can sting its victim again and again.

Scary Insects

In 2019, extra-large hornets arrived in North America. People called them "murder hornets."

Hornets are dangerous to bees in two ways. Because a hornet is so big and fierce, it can easily kill a worker bee. Then, it brings the bee's body back to its hive. It feeds the dead bee to its hornet larvae.

Hornets will also take all the honey out of a hive. They will bring it home to feed the other hornets and larvae.

A Fight to the Death

Let's check back with the beehive. The bees know that a swarm of hornets is coming to attack them. What will the hornets do next? They rush into the beehive. They use their strong jaws to bite off the heads of the worker bees.

The bees know they cannot stop the hornets from breaking into their hive. But they need to protect the queen and the honey in the hive. So, they have another plan.

They gather in a big ball. They vibrate their wings. When the hornets enter the nest, they are in for a big surprise. The bees surround the hornets. The hornets are trapped inside the bee ball. What happens next?

Vibrating their wings makes the hive very hot. The bees don't mind the heat. But the hornets do! The hornets can't escape the ball of bees. It's so hot, the hornets are actually cooked to death.

Not all the hornets are trapped inside the ball. They attack the bees. They bite off the bees' heads. What will happen next? Think about each animal's weapons and defenses. Then, you decide! Who do you think will win this deadly battle?

Shimmer and Shine

Scientists have seen honeybees gathering in large groups outside their hive. The bees flash their bellies. This light can scare hornets and other predators away.

Honeybee vs. Hornet

Range of Honeybee

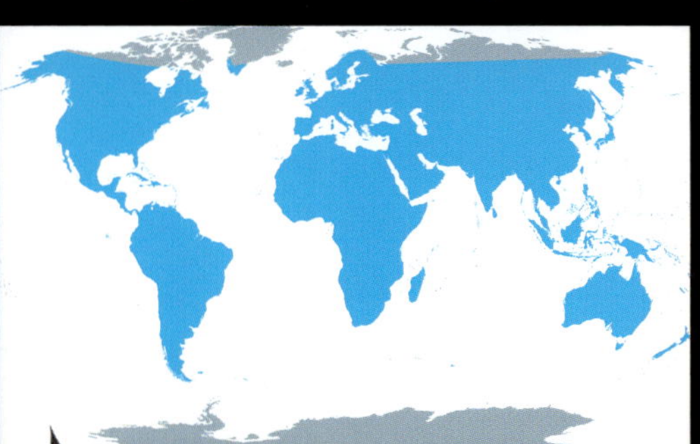

Range of Hornet

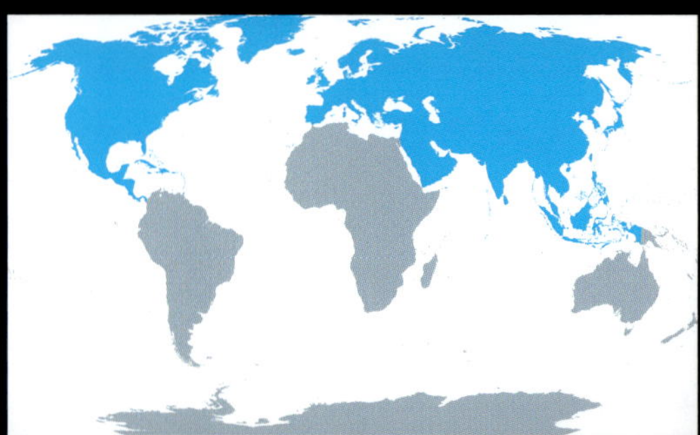

Let's Compare

Honeybee: Weight—About 0.0035 ounces (100 mg); Length—About 0.6 inch (15 mm)

Hornet: Weight—up to one ounce (28 grams); Length—up to 2.2 inches (5.5 cm)

Honeybee: Small, barbed stinger with venom; can only sting once

Hornet: Long stinger with venom; can sting again and again

Honeybee: Stinger and venom

Hornet: Stinger and venom; large, powerful jaws

Honeybee: Can vibrate their wings to make the hive very hot

Hornet: Gather in large groups to attack enemies

abdomen (AB-duh-muhn)
the segment at the end of an insect's body

larvae (LAHR-vee)
insects at the stage of development between an egg and a pupa, when it looks worm-like

nectar (NEK-tur)
a sweet liquid found inside some flowers

organs (OR-guhnz)
parts of the body, such as the brain or heart

pollen (PAH-luhn)
tiny yellow grains produced by flowers

predator (PRED-uh-tur)
an animal that hunts and eats other animals

scout (SKOWT)
someone sent to find out and bring back information

stinger (STING-ur)
a sharp body part that can inject venom

venom sac (VEHN-uhm SAK)
part of an insect's body that contains poison

vibrate (VYE-brate)
to move back and forth very quickly

1. Hornets mark beehives with a special ________.
   A. smell B. sound C. symbol

2. All worker bees are ________.
   A. male B. female C. queens

3. Hornets can sting ________.
   A. once B. twice C. many times

4. Bees vibrate their wings to make the hive very ________.
   A. noisy B. crowded C. hot

Answers
1. A, 2. B, 3. C, 4. C

BOOKS

Becker, Trudy. *Giant Hornets*. Focus Readers, 2023.

Klepeis, Alicia. *Asian Giant Hornets*. Jump!, 2023.

Neye, Emily. *Honeybees*. Random House Books for Young Readers, 2016.

ON THE INTERNET

A-to-Z Animals: Hornet
a-z-animals.com/animals/hornet/
This webpage features lots of facts, photos, and more about hornets.

Britannica: Hornet
www.britannica.com/animal/hornet-insect
This article includes interesting facts about hornets, where they live, and what their lives are like.

National Geographic Kids: 10 Facts About Honeybees!
www.natgeokids.com/au/discover/animals/insects/honey-bees/
Learn some fascinating facts about honeybees with National Geographic Kids.

Nature Mapping Animal Facts For Kids: Honey Bee
naturemappingfoundation.org/natmap/facts/honey_bee_k6.html
This webpage has fun facts and photos about honeybees.

Index

About the Author

Joanne Mattern has written many nonfiction books for children. She adores animals of all kinds. Although Joanne thinks hornets are very scary, she was fascinated to learn more about them, as well as about honeybees, while writing this book. Joanne lives in New York State with her family.